ANOTHER LOOK
AT THE
BEGINNING

ANOTHER LOOK AT THE BEGINNING

ANTHONY MALE

authorHOUSE®

AuthorHouse™ UK Ltd.
1663 Liberty Drive
Bloomington, IN 47403 USA
www.authorhouse.co.uk
Phone: 0800.197.4150

All my quotations come from the Authorised King James' Bible

Published by AuthorHouse 12/13/2013

ISBN: 978-1-4918-8797-4 (sc)
ISBN: 978-1-4918-8796-7 (hc)
ISBN: 978-1-4918-8798-1 (e)

INTRODUCTION

For as long as I can remember, I have been fascinated by the story of the Creation as told in the Bible. I decided to look at that story word by word to see what it actually says. Many of the major events of the Bible are covered in a very few words and so the meaning of each word becomes very important.

To many, the Creation as told in Genesis is just a fairy story and the excitement of trying to prove great scientific theories has taken up much time and money. None of the theories has ever been proved, since there were no eye witness accounts, and none of them have overcome the problem that there had to be a space and some matter before it could all get started.

I have chosen the Authorised King James' version as the script on which to base my writing. The new translations of the Bible do not disagree with the sense of it and it is a beautiful script with which to work. Whatever you believe about how we all landed up here and now, I hope that you will enjoy this exploration.

Anthony Male.

THE FIRST BOOK OF MOSES, CALLED

GENESIS.

CHAPTER ONE

Verse 1. IN the beginning God created the heaven and the earth.

'In the beginning'. In the beginning of our future environment. The story relates to man and earthly creation. God was already there, larger than the heaven which he had created. In this statement he had created two things; the heaven and the earth. It does not say that the earth was in it's position in the heaven at this stage. Looking backwards, it would seem that God created an environment into which the earth could be put. It reminds me of a gardener preparing a carboy for planting, as one would a bottle garden. The necessary elements for the garden come from outside of the bottle but are then placed within the environment of the bottle to create the garden.

Verse 2. And the earth was without form, and void; and darkness *was* upon the face of the deep. And the spirit of God moved upon the face of the waters.

So here it is, this splodge of matter, shapeless and barren but wet. We are not considering the sphere as it has been known in modern times. There is no rotary movement around a sun to promote the formation of a spherical shape. At this stage there is no sun, just the heaven and the earth. A large lump of substance with, perhaps, a deep fissure in it and water, but already the Spirit of God is there, moving upon the face of that water.

Verse 3. And God said, Let there be light: and there was light.

Back now to the bottle garden scenario. A space called 'heaven' made ready to take the lump of matter and water called earth. The earth is not yet ready to be put into the heaven and needs work to be done in preparation. God calls for light in the same way, perhaps, that a scientist would call for more light in a laboratory; to see more clearly to carry out the task in view. This light is therefore some form of God's light. It is the light available to God's environment, it is not from the sun in a created heaven. The created heaven does not have any light of it's own as yet. This seems to be laboratory lighting, God's laboratory.

Verse 4. And God saw the light, that *it was* good: and God divided the light from the darkness.

We now have this splodge with a directed light upon it, but the light is shining upon it for a time and then removed so that we have a day and night set of circumstances. We are told that God is pleased with the arrangement.

Verse 5. And God called the light Day, and the darkness he called Night. And the evening and the morning were the first day.

Already Day and Night have names but the earth has not yet been placed into it's heaven, the light of the first day comes from God and not from a created Sun. This situation throws up another important matter and that is the subject of time. The first day was calculated in God's heavenly time, not solar time. It is therefore logical to suppose that all of the elements of the Creation story are to be considered in God's heavenly days. It certainly gives time for the coming and passing of the dinosaurs and the other facets of the Earth's evolvement. We seem to be saying then, that whilst our solar system and all the universe as we know it, are in heaven, it is a heaven that God has made within a heaven. Therefore in the bottle garden scenario, the carboy is stood within another environment loosely given the same name. Our universe is a contained entity placed within a much larger setting. God is huge!

Verse 6. And God said, Let there be a firmament in the midst of the waters, and let it divide the waters from the waters.

Verse 7. And God made the firmament, and divided the waters which *were* under the firmament from the waters which *were* above the firmament: and it was so.

Here we have the environment of the earth as a given quantity. There is no more substance added, the water from the splodge is separated out, just as the rain is drawn up by the sun into the formation of clouds today. Whilst, however, the principle is put into practise, the eventual means of so doing has not yet been created.

Verse 8. And God called the firmament Heaven. And the evening and the morning were the second day.

Day two in God's heavenly time and we have the meaning of the word 'Heaven' defined as the space between the waters on the splodge and the waters separated to above the splodge. 'Heaven', therefore, means space. We have heaven between us and the clouds, we have heaven outside of this area and we have heaven outside of the area of the universe in which God is making His creation.

Verse 9. And God said, Let the waters under the heaven be gathered together unto one place, and let the dry *land* appear: and it was so.

The concept of separate dry and wet areas is God's intention; it could have been all one wet bog.

Verse 10. And God called the dry *land* Earth; and the gathering together of the waters called he Seas: and God saw that *it was* good.

One can imagine the Spirit of God moving upon the face of the waters as in verse two, and moulding the seas into shape.

Verse 11. And God said, Let the earth bring forth grass, the herb yielding seed, *and* the fruit tree

yielding fruit after his kind, whose seed *is* in itself, upon the earth: and it was so.

The nature of these plants is individual, there is grass, the herb which produces seed and then the fruit with the seeds enclosed within it. The other piece of information here is that the plants are brought forth from the earth and so the splodge has already been planted with seeds, whilst the earth is in it's laboratory situation. They are specific types of plant, each with a different nature in their growth.

Verse 12. And the earth brought forth grass, *and* herb yielding seed after his kind, and the tree yielding fruit, whose seed *was* in itself, after his kind: and God saw that *it was* good.

The earth and plants are responding to God's will. God has created the situation and the life to grow into that situation. Here we have confirmation that it is actually happening as God had intended, but the set up is still in a laboratory location.

Verse 13. And the evening and the morning were the third day.

The sun has not yet been created.

Verse 14. And God said, Let there be lights in the firmament of the heaven to divide the day from the night; and let them be for signs, and for seasons, and for days, and years:

The laboratory experiment has worked and now comes the time to set up the support systems within the environment into which the earth is to be placed. There is now a means of providing day and night and a means of calculating earthly years.

Verse 15. And let them be for lights in the firmament of the heaven to give light upon the earth: and it was so.

Verse 16. And God made two great lights; the greater light to rule the day, and the lesser light to rule the night: *he made* **the stars also.**

It is an interesting use of the word rule because when considered, the factor of quantity of light does determine what we are able to do. The fact that the sun produces the light and the moon reflects it is irrelevant when we consider that the result is light to us. Also we have no understanding of the nature of God's light. The light from Moses' face when he came down from the mountain was more than people could tolerate according to Exodus Chapter 34 verses 29-35.

Verse 17. And God set them in the firmament of the heaven to give light upon the earth,

The earth, sun, moon and other heavenly bodies are set in their places.

Verse 18. And to rule over the day and over the night, and to divide the light from the darkness: and God saw that *it was* good.

Verse 19. And the evening and the morning were the fourth day.

Everything is now set up. There is sea and dry land, which is already planted. There is a means of continuing the laboratory conditions by use of the sun.

Verse 20. And God said, Let the waters bring forth abundantly the moving creature that hath life, and fowl *that* may fly above the earth in the open firmament of heaven.

Verse 21. And God created great whales, and every living creature that moveth, which the waters brought

forth abundantly, after their kind, and every winged fowl after his kind: and God saw that *it was* good.

Again each creation after it's own kind.

Verse 22. And God blessed them, saying, Be fruitful, and multiply, and fill the waters in the seas, and let fowl multiply in the earth.

A wonderful earth, with sea creatures and birds. God wants them to multiply and to fill the waters and the earth. Reproduction is a wonderful process created by God.

Verse 23. And the evening and the morning were the fifth day.

There is no mention of any kind of change in the Biblical reckoning of the length of the days and so we must continue to suppose that we are still in heavenly time, rather than in solar time.

Verse 24. And God said, Let the earth bring forth the living creature after his kind, cattle, and creeping thing, and beast of the earth after his kind: and it was so.

This is interesting, because here we have the creatures, presumably created from the earth. It is the earth which is to let to bring forth. Every creation, however, is still specific, 'After his kind'.

Verse 25. And God made the beast of the earth after his kind, and cattle after their kind, and every thing that creepeth upon the earth after his kind: and God saw that *it was* good.

Here the previous verse is expounded, explaining that God is the maker of the animals and that the beast, the cattle and everything that creepeth upon the earth are each made after their own kind.

Verse 26. And God said, Let us make man in our image, after our likeness: and let them have dominion over the fish of the sea, and over the fowl of the air, and over the cattle, and over all the earth, and over every creeping thing that creepeth upon the earth.

Here we have a definite decision by God to make man. It is not a development, but a decision to create man 'in our image'. Here also is the use of the Royal 'our', or is it plural? Are there other beings in God's image in the greater heaven? Man is to be given power; he is to have dominion over all of the creatures, indeed over all of the earth.

Verse 27. So God created man in his *own* image, in the image of God created he him; male and female created he them.

There is an interesting point here and that is the use of the word man. Back in verse 26, God has put man in charge of the earth but it infers that it is not just one man but mankind. Could, therefore, the man in verse 27 also be plural so that we have a body of people, male and female, to start off the population of the earth?

Verse 28. And God blessed them, and God said unto them, Be fruitful, and multiply, and replenish the earth, and subdue it: and have dominion over the fish of the sea, and over the fowl of the air, and over every living thing that moveth upon the earth.

Nothing here to clash with the single or plural theory. The word 'replenish' is interesting, it does not seem to appear in some other translations and yet it infers a history of something happening so that the earth had to be renewed in some way. Could there have been a previous disaster, perhaps, including the death of the dinosaurs?

Verse 29. And God said, Behold, I have given you every herb bearing seed, which *is* upon the face of all

the earth, and every tree, in the which *is* the fruit of a tree yielding seed; to you it shall be for meat.

Here God is giving dietary information. A diet that would still be regarded as healthy today.

Verse 30. And to every beast of the earth, and to every fowl of the air, and to every thing that creepeth upon the earth, wherein *there is* life, *I have given* every green herb for meat: and it was so.

This is to be the animal's diet.

Verse 31. And God saw every thing that he had made, and, behold, *it was* very good. And the evening and the morning were the sixth day.

Here God is looking back upon his work from an outside viewpoint and it is not only the Earth, but the entire Universe. The bottle garden scenario of the Universe, our Solar System and the planet Earth. The

Earth is now planted and populated with animals and man, both male and female. Whilst Adam and Eve were the first of humankind, there is nothing in the text to say that there were not others made by God, indeed all the evidence later shows that there may have been.

CHAPTER TWO

Verse 1. THUS the heavens and the earth were finished, and all the host of them.

This is a summary and confirmation of the preceding chapter. There is one interesting word and that is 'host'. Host here not only seems to cover mankind but also animal life. Does the word when used in other parts of the Bible also include animal life?

Verse 2. And on the seventh day God ended his work which he had made; and he rested on the seventh day from all his work which he had made.

The extraordinary factor here is that God took a rest after work. This is an early confirmation, perhaps, that we are made in God's own image. Also the work is very personal to God; it is God's own work.

Verse 3. And God blessed the seventh day, and sanctified it: because that in it he had rested from all his work which God created and made.

Rest is a blessing that is sanctified.

Verse 4. These *are* the generations of the heavens and of the earth when they were created, in the day that the LORD God made the earth and the heavens,

Once again, the Earth and the Heavens are spoken of as separate creations.

Verse 5. And every plant of the field before it was in the earth, and every herb of the field before it grew: for the LORD God had not caused it to rain upon the earth, and *there was* not a man to till the ground.

Notice the statement, 'before it was in the earth', and then think back to Chapter 1. verse 11. and that the seeds were planted in a wet splodge before the solar system was made. The opening statement of this verse somehow ties in with that. These individual families of vegetation were part of the creation whilst at laboratory stage and they were of individual type, not a product of evolution.

Verse 6. But there went up a mist from the earth, and watered the whole face of the ground.

The water was part of the package, a self sufficient entity of so much solid and so much wet, put together before it gradually was caused to separate out; just like under watering a seed tray. All the water at this stage would therefore, presumably, have been fresh rather than salt water.

Verse 7. And the LORD God formed man *of* the dust of the ground, and breathed into his nostrils the breath of life; and man became a living soul.

This is interesting because plants came from heavenly seeds that were put into the earth before it was placed into the solar system. Man is a much later addition, or rather no addition at all, since he is made from the substance of the earth. It is only when the breath of God is put into him that he becomes a living soul. We all, therefore, have this element of God within us, whether we recognise it or not.

Verse 8. And the LORD God planted a garden eastward in Eden; and there he put the man whom he had formed.

Now we have a place particularly planted by God for the sustenance and pleasure of Man. It is a garden and not a wilderness.

Verse 9. And out of the ground made the LORD God to grow every tree that is pleasant to the sight, and good for food; the tree of life also in the midst of the garden, and the tree of knowledge of good and evil.

Here is a place where there is beauty and the trees are pleasant to the sight. There is food here, good food. It does not give a reason in the Bible why God plants two trees which are so special: The Tree of Life and The Tree of Knowledge of Good and Evil. Whilst The Tree of Life seems, perhaps, in keeping, The Tree of Knowledge of Good and Evil seems somehow extraordinary, in that this knowledge should be contained within a tree. There is also the indication that there is good and there is evil and there is the knowledge of the difference between them. Perhaps it is an irony that we now have books full of knowledge that are made from trees!

Verse 10. And a river went out of Eden to water the garden; and from thence it was parted, and became into four heads.

It is a riverside garden with fresh, not salt, water because the water irrigates the garden. This is the first clue as to the whereabouts of the place today.

Verse 11. The name of the first *is* Pison: that *is* it which compasseth the whole land of Havilah, where *there is* gold;

We now have a detailed geographical location of the Garden of Eden. There is also a precious metal: gold.

Verse 12. And the gold of that land *is* good: there *is* bdellium and the onyx stone.

This has been written at a time when comparison could be made between gold here and gold in other places.

Verse 13. And the name of the second river *is* Gihon: the same *is* it that compasseth the whole land of Ethiopia.

More geographical details and the river is identified with Ethiopia.

Verse 14. And the name of the third river *is* Hiddekel: that *is* it which goeth toward the east of Assyria. And the fourth river *is* Euphrates.

The Euphrates is still here today after thousands of years including the time of the Flood.

Verse 15. And the LORD God took the man, and put him into the garden of Eden to dress it and to keep it.

Man has been given a custodial role in God's creation.

Verse 16. And the LORD God commanded the man, saying, Of every tree of the garden thou mayest freely eat:

This was a garden, not a wild place; there are no poisonous or harmful plants here.

Verse 17. But the tree of the knowledge of good and evil, thou shalt not eat of it: for in the day that thou eatest thereof thou shalt surely die.

This is a surprising verse considering that it is a tree in which the knowledge of good and evil is accessible. It is, however, an accurate prediction in that by the eating of this; mankind would then suffer the experience of death. The text does not say that, thou shalt surely die immediately. Does it perhaps mean death as a form of separation from his previous relationship with God and then physical death of the body?

Verse 18. And the LORD God said, *It is* not good that the man should be alone; I will make him an help meet for him.

The concern and love of God shows itself here. Here is individual man and an individual human, suitable for being a mate for the man, is going to be created especially for him.

Verse 19. And out of the ground the LORD God formed every beast of the field, and every fowl of the air; and brought *them* unto Adam to see what he would call them: and whatsoever Adam called every living creature, that *was* the name thereof.

This verse shows the position in which God holds man, as being above the other creatures. Man is to give them names, they are made from the earth and so they are the same substance as Man but Man has a position above them.

Verse 20. And Adam gave names to all cattle, and to the fowl of the air, and to every beast of the field; but for Adam there was not found an help meet for him.

Adam was not to find his partner in creation thus far, the animal kingdom was separate.

Verse 21. And the LORD God caused a deep sleep to fall upon Adam, and he slept: and he took one of his ribs, and closed up the flesh instead thereof;

This is the first operation on Earth. The idea of a sleep whilst the work was being carried out is still very relevant today. There were probably no anaesthetics used at the time when Genesis was written, so this is inspired writing.

Verse 22. And the rib, which the LORD God had taken from man, made he a woman, and brought her unto the man.

With our modern knowledge of medicine and cloning this does not seem too far fetched. Consider, however, the scribes who believed this through faith alone, without our modern understanding of medical science. How wonderful the faith of our forefathers and how beyond the imagination of that age, to invent such a story. Now it seems quite possible that Eve could have been created in this way, but our ancestors had to believe through faith alone.

Verse 23. And Adam said, This *is* now bone of my bones, and flesh of my flesh: she shall be called Woman, because she was taken out of Man.

God could have created a woman in the same way as He had created a man but He chose to make woman from the rib of the man that He had already created. A twist perhaps that helps to give strength to the argument that the scriptures are inspired and not a thought up story, by some clever writer.

Verse 24. Therefore shall a man leave his father and his mother, and shall cleave unto his wife: and they shall be one flesh.

This verse before any form of human conception, birth or other humans with whom to relate. Every aspect of the creation process has been carefully planned to produce results.

Verse 25. And they were both naked, the man and his wife, and were not ashamed.

Two points here. Nakedness is our natural state and beautiful for God since He made us and we are all His creation. The relationship of a man and a woman being together was in itself considered as marriage. In a way Eve had been given to Adam as a father gives his daughter away at a wedding, but there was no official ceremony and they were both virgins.

CHAPTER THREE

Verse 1. NOW the serpent was more subtil than any beast of the field which the LORD God had made. And he said unto the woman, Yea, hath God said, Ye shall not eat of every tree of the garden?

The serpent was made by God and had more subtlety than any of the other animals that God had made. What is more he was able to communicate with mankind.

Verse 2. And the woman said unto the serpent, We may eat of the fruit of the trees of the garden:

The diet is a fruit diet and perhaps seeds and nuts.

Verse 3. But of the fruit of the tree which *is* in the midst of the garden, God hath said, Ye shall not eat of it, neither shall ye touch it, lest ye die.

The woman was knowledgeable about what and what not could be eaten according to God's will. It is interesting that the fruit was not to be touched. The result was to be death. The meaning of death was understood but no human had yet died.

Verse 4. And the serpent said unto the woman, Ye shall not surely die:

There is an ambiguous view of death here. The woman would appear to be thinking of death as an instant striking down and it is on this that the serpent plays. Perhaps, however, death would never have been known to man at all had it not been for the act of disobedience which was about to be committed. Perhaps it meant the death of a closeness with God which had up to now existed and which did not reoccur generally with large numbers until the coming of the Holy Spirit at Pentecost. There was, however, the threat of a real change about to take place if the act of disobedience happened.

Verse 5. For God doth know that in the day ye eat thereof, then your eyes shall be opened, and ye shall be as gods, knowing good and evil.

So here we have death which is not immediate but the promise of death which does come eventually. The serpent also knows the properties of the fruit of the tree. What happened if the animals ate of the fruit? The serpent is aware of higher beings in his reference to gods. He also relates to God as above these higher beings in the way that the text is worded.

Verse 6. And when the woman saw that the tree *was* good for food, and that it *was* pleasant to the eyes, and a tree to be desired to make *one* wise, she took the fruit thereof, and did eat, and gave also unto her husband with her; and he did eat.

How often are we tempted to eat food because of it's appearance? Adam is referred to as 'husband', could this mean that they had already discovered each other sexually? There is no mention of a ceremony or formal arrangement but they could be regarded as man and wife.

Verse 7. And the eyes of them both were opened, and they knew that they *were* naked; and they sewed fig leaves together, and made themselves aprons.

Up until now they had been blissful in their ignorance, but now they looked at things in a different way. The work of the sewing must have been a new discovery; there would have been no need to have done this before.

Verse 8. And they heard the voice of the LORD God walking in the garden in the cool of the day: and Adam and his wife hid themselves from the presence of the LORD God amongst the trees of the garden.

It would now seem to be evening time and Adam and Eve are aware of the presence of God and they know that they have done wrong, so they hide.

Verse 9. And the LORD God called unto Adam, and said unto him, Where *art* thou?

The relationship is very personal

Verse 10. And he said, I heard thy voice in the garden, and I was afraid, because I *was* naked; and I hid myself.

Again the use of 'Thy' rather than 'Your', expresses the closeness of the relationship. Adam's sin is exposed and he makes a futile attempt to hide his wrongdoing.

Verse 11. And he said, Who told thee that thou *wast* naked? Hast thou eaten of the tree, whereof I commanded thee that thou shouldest not eat?

A straightforward question. Is this physical or spiritual nakedness?

Verse 12. And the man said, The woman whom you gavest *to be* with me, she gave me of the tree, and I did eat.

Adam is frightened and his wife and partner now becomes, 'The woman'.

Verse 13. And the LORD God said unto the woman, What *is* this *that* thou hast done? And the woman said, The serpent beguiled me, and I did eat.

Eve is also frightened and passes the blame onto the serpent.

Verse 14. And the LORD God said unto the serpent, Because thou hast done this, thou *art* cursed above all cattle, and above every beast of the field; upon thy belly shalt thou go, and dust shalt thou eat all the days of thy life:

The clever serpent became too precocious and is reduced to the bottom of the animal order. Perhaps this creature became wormlike.

Verse 15. And I will put enmity between thee and the woman, and between thy seed and her seed; it shall bruise thy head, and thou shalt bruise his heel.

Interesting use of, 'his' rather than, 'her' relating to the heel. Many people today do not like snakes and worms.

Verse 16. Unto the woman he said, I will greatly multiply thy sorrow and thy conception; in sorrow thou shalt bring forth children; and thy desire *shall be* to thy husband, and he shall rule over thee.

God designed women to have children but the process is now to be less enjoyable than it might have been. The relationship between men and women has been set up.

Verse 17. And unto Adam he said, Because thou has hearkened unto the voice of thy wife, and hast eaten of the tree, of which I commanded thee, saying, Thou shalt not eat of it: cursed *is* the ground for thy sake; in sorrow shalt thou eat *of* it all the days of thy life;

Adam had listened to his wife rather than following God's command. The joyous abundance is still there but in his sorrow Adam cannot now fully enjoy it.

Verse 18. Thorns also and thistles shall it bring forth to thee; and thou shalt eat the herb of the field;

Eden was a garden planted by God with all the beautiful and choice foods for Adam and Eve to enjoy. Before disobeying God they are not aware of other less beautiful vegetation, the thorns and plants that grow outside of this paradise. Now they are to experience them directly. Their diet is also to change from tree bearing, easy to pick and eat food to the vegetation closer to the ground.

Verse 19. In the sweat of thy face shalt thou eat bread, till thou return unto the ground; for out of it wast thou taken: for dust thou *art,* and unto dust shalt thou return.

Adam is brought down to size. He will work now for his food and will eventually return to the dust from which he was made. It is God's power alone that can make him any being else.

Verse 20. And Adam called his wife's name Eve; because she was the mother of all living.

At this stage Eve is the first lady. Mother here is a social title rather than a physical statistic, at this time she had not yet conceived.

Verse 21. Unto Adam also and to his wife did the LORD God make coats of skins, and clothed them.

Adam and Eve are about to be expelled from the paradise that God had made for them. They will need protection from the elements and from the thorns.

Verse 22. And the LORD God said, Behold, the man is become as one of us, to know good and evil: and now, lest he put forth his hand, and take also of the tree of life, and eat, and live for ever:

Adam and Eve had gone against God's will once, they might do it again.

Verse 23. Therefore the LORD God sent him forth from the garden of Eden, to till the ground from whence he was taken.

Man has now to work for his food.

Verse 24. So he drove out the man; and he placed at the east of the garden of Eden Cherubims, and a

flaming sword which turned every way, to keep the way of the tree of life.

Even at this time the East has an importance, and we have Cherubims mentioned. The tree of life is protected by something sharing a similar description as how we might describe a laser, it is effective.

CHAPTER FOUR

Verse 1. AND Adam knew Eve his wife; and she conceived, and bare Cain, and said, I have gotten a man from the LORD.

Procreation begins. Adam and Eve, although cast out, still relate to God and know that they are receiving this blessing from God.

Verse 2. And she again bare his brother Abel. And Abel was a keeper of sheep, but Cain was a tiller of the ground.

A long period covered in a few short words: another son and now grown up, they have careers.

Verse 3. And in the process of time it came to pass, that Cain brought of the fruit of the ground an offering unto the LORD.

The relationship continues in the second generation and the first offering is given back to God.

Verse 4. And Abel, he also brought of the firstlings of his flock and of the fat thereof. And the LORD had respect unto Abel and to his offering:

Mixed Farming, God is pleased with the offering that Abel has brought. Abel has brought a firstling and one of the best of the flock, a requirement of God often mentioned in the law concerning sacrifices later on.

Verse 5. But unto Cain and to his offering he had not respect. And Cain was very wroth, and his countenance fell.

Cain was the firstborn and brought the first offering, but God preferred the offering of his younger brother, Abel. Cain is upset.

Verse 6. And the LORD said unto Cain, Why art thou wroth? And why is thy countenance fallen?

God perceives the change of attitude and asks why.

Verse 7. If thou doest well, shalt thou not be accepted? and if thou doest not well, sin lieth at the door. And unto thee *shall be* his desire, and thou shalt rule over him.

One must always do their best, otherwise it is easy to become sidetracked into sinful ways. When one is purposefully doing one's best, then one is the master of the situation.

Verse 8. And Cain talked with Abel his brother: and it came to pass, when they were in the field, that Cain rose up against Abel his brother, and slew him.

The first murder and obviously cold blooded and brought about by jealously. Cain spoke with Abel rather than fight with him. Cain is jealous and cannot contain his feelings of resentment. He kills his only brother.

Verse 9. And the LORD said unto Cain, Where *is* Abel thy brother? And he said, I know not: *Am* I my brother's keeper?

The first human death on earth but God does not intervene to prevent it. He asks Cain in a calm but penetrating way.

Verse 10. And he said, What hast thou done? the voice of thy brother's blood crieth unto me from the ground.

The knowledge of the individual condition, which God has of all His creation.

Verse 11. And now *art* thou cursed from the earth, which hath opened her mouth to receive thy brother's blood from thy hand;

The curse comes from the earth and not from God. It is human earthly blood that has been shed.

Verse 12. When thou tillest the ground, it shall not henceforth yield unto thee her strength; a fugitive and a vagabond shalt thou be in the earth.

Adam and Eve were cast out from the Garden of Eden and now Cain is to also suffer punishment. If he does farm then he will not receive the best from the ground, and so it seems that his lot will be to wander like a fugitive. The comfort that they once enjoyed has been taken from them because of their going against God's will, the price of sin.

Verse 13. And Cain said unto the LORD, My punishment *is* greater than I can bear.

The contact with God is still there. God has not abandoned him.

Verse 14. Behold, thou hast driven me out this day from the face of the earth; and from thy face shall I be hid; and I shall be a fugitive and a vagabond in the earth; and it shall come to pass, *that* every one that findeth me shall slay me.

It seems that Cain is to be sent away from those who are known to him in his surrounding world or earth as he names it. There would seem to be more than Adam and Eve in this consideration. Cain believes that he will be hidden from God's face now and he speaks of those who find him, killing him. Where do these other people come from? Although the Bible says that God made Adam and then Eve, it does not say that they were the only people who He made. The children of Adam and Eve are clearly named and that would seem to rule out a crowd situation within one generation. There seem to be fellow humans about at the same time and it could be that they were also children of other couples created immediately after Adam and Eve.

Verse 15. And the LORD said unto him, Therefore whosoever slayeth Cain, vengeance shall be taken on him sevenfold. And the LORD set a mark upon Cain, lest any finding him should kill him.

Again the reference to other people and people who recognise the power of God. They would recognise the mark being put upon Cain's head as God's mark and they would be too afraid of God to harm Cain.

Verse 16. And Cain went out from the presence of the LORD, and dwelt in the land of Nod, on the east of Eden.

The perception that Cain was leaving God's presence must have signified Cain's own spiritual crisis at that time. If the people to whom he was going would be able to recognise God's mark on him, then they were God fearing people. God is everywhere, but it is, perhaps, Cain's feeling of guilt that is beginning to weigh upon him and separate him from God in his own mind.

Verse 17. And Cain knew his wife; and she conceived, and bare Enoch: and he builded a city, and called the name of the city, after the name of his son, Enoch.

Nod is not a barren place, there are other people, enough to fill a city, and Cain must be of some standing to be able to organise the building of such a place to celebrate the birth of his son. Where did Cain's wife come from, was she from the tribe of Nod? Perhaps Cain has been repentant, God seems to have forgiven him and blessed him, he seems to have found great happiness again, and acceptance in the company of God fearing people.

Verse 18. And unto Enoch was born Irad: and Irad begat Mehujael: and Mehujael begat Methusael: and Methusael begat Lamech.

This is the beginning of Cain's dynasty. There is imagination or inspiration concerning the formation of names. Only the male heirs are named in the Bible.

Verse 19. And Lamech took unto him two wives: the name of the one *was* Adah, and the name of the other Zillah.

More girls, presumably, from other families. Cain went out from his own family area and so God must have created other people immediately after Adam and Eve in other areas, otherwise their children would not have been available to have married Adam and Eve's children.

Verse 20. And Adah bare Jabal: he was father of such as dwell in tents, and *of such as have* cattle.

Cain seems to be a town type but Jabel seems to be the beginning of the great nomadic tradition of herders moving the animals according to the availability of grazing pasture.

Verse 21. And his brother's name *was* Jubal: he was the father of all such as handle the harp and organ.

Culture has arrived with musical instruments, the first mention of the arts.

Verse 22. And Zillah, she also bare Tubal-Cain, an instructor of every artificer in brass and iron: and the sister of Tubal-Cain *was* Naamah.

Manufacturing and processing has begun. Life was perfectly possible for years without any form of metallic processing, some form of inspiration must have given early man the need to progress in this way. The step of taking unrelated raw materials, extracting part of their substance, subjecting them to a previously unknown process and attaining something with quite different potential could not have been an accident.

Verse 23. And Lamech said unto his wives, Adah and Zillah, Hear my voice; ye wives of Lamech, harken unto my speech: for I have slain a man to my wounding, and a young man to my hurt.

Apparently fighting and violence are as close as ever. Lamech realises that in killing someone, he has harmed something within himself. Since the man was young, with the hope of much life ahead, this has in some way made the hurt much greater to Lamech himself.

Verse 24. If Cain shall be avenged sevenfold, truly Lamech seventy and sevenfold.

Family history has been passed down through the generations.

Verse 25. And Adam knew his wife again; and she bare a son, and called his name Seth: For God, *said she,* hath appointed me another seed instead of Abel, whom Cain slew.

Here we find that the generations are still all alive, but we are not told how much contact there is between the branches of the family and how far apart they are living. In Eve's mind, Seth is a replacement for Abel. This statement further supports the theory that God created other humans after Adam and Eve, and who with their descendents formed part of the human population. Since the children of Adam and Eve seem to be named and recorded, then it would appear that the other people to whom the text refers must have been created independently. God is constant and the idea of sexual relationships between brothers and sisters does not seem a likely part of the plan.

Verse 26. And to Seth, to him also there was born a son; and he called his name Enos: then began men to call upon the name of the LORD.

This would appear to be the beginning of a new relationship with God, perhaps the beginning of worship?

CHAPTER FIVE

Verse 1. THIS *is* the book of the generations of Adam. In the day that God created man, in the likeness of God made he him;

God could have chosen to make man in any form but he chose to make him in his own likeness.

Verse 2. Male and female created he them; and blessed them, and called their name Adam, in the day when they were created.

The name Adam not only relates to the first man but also to mankind, male and female.

Verse 3. And Adam lived an hundred and thirty years, and begat *a son* in his own likeness, after his image; and called his name Seth:

When he was a hundred and thirty years old he sired a son who was like him. Interesting that Seth was described as being like his father, perhaps Cain and Abel were like their mother.

Verse 4. And the days of Adam after he had begotten Seth were eight hundred years: and he begat sons and daughters:

Adam and presumably Eve lived a long time and were able to produce children in their old age. We do not know their diet or lifestyle but everything was pure, unpolluted and probably eaten raw. We do not know the speed of the earth around the sun at this time: the universe was younger then, years may have been shorter or longer than today.

Verse 5. And all the days that Adam lived were nine hundred and thirty years: and he died.

Adam was a man made by God and he died in the way that men die.

Verse 6. And Seth lived an hundred and five years, and begat Enos:

Seth was one hundred and five years old when he sired Enos. Perhaps he was a late developer or perhaps he had not found a woman, we do not know how far apart people were living or the dangers in trying to meet other people. Perhaps he had fathered girls and this was the first boy and so he was recorded.

Verse 7. And Seth lived after he begat Enos eight hundred and seven years, and begat sons and daughters:

It does not say how many wives Enos had and only the firstborn male is named in the text.

Verse 8. And all the days of Seth were nine hundred and twelve years: and he died.

Seth was born of a man and a woman, unlike Adam and Eve, but he still has a similar lifespan.

Verse 9. And Enos lived ninety years, and begat Cainan:

The name incorporates the name 'Cain'.

Verse 10. And Enos lived after he begat Cainan eight hundred and fifteen years, and begat sons and daughters:

Verse 11. And all the days of Enos were nine hundred and five years: and he died.

Verse 12. And Cainan lived seventy years, and Begat Mahalaleel:

Cainan seems to be younger than the others when he starts a family, or is it that the others had girls first, who were not named in the text?

Verse 13. And Cainan lived after he begat Mahalaleel eight hundred and forty years, and begat sons and daughters:

Again only the name of the first son is given.

Verse 14. And all the days of Cainan were nine hundred and ten years: and he died.

Verse 15. And Mahalaleel lived sixty and five years, and begat Jared:

Another young starter.

Verse 16. And Mahalaleel lived after he begat Jared eight hundred and thirty years, and begat sons and daughters:

Verse 17. And all the days of Mahalaleel were eight hundred ninety and five years: and he died.

Verse 18. And Jared lived an hundred sixty and two years, and he begat Enoch:

Much later again, unless he sired girls beforehand.

Verse 19. And Jared lived after he begat Enoch eight hundred years, and begat sons and daughters:

Verse 20. And all the days of Jared were nine hundred sixty and two years: and he died.

Verse 21. And Enoch lived sixty and five years, and begat Methuselah:

Verse 22. And Enoch walked with God after he begat Methuselah three hundred years, and begat sons and daughters:

Verse 23. And all the days of Enoch were three hundred sixty and five years:

Verse 24. And Enoch walked with God: and he *was* not; for God took him.

This is an extraordinary statement because apparently Enoch did not die, but went to God as he was. It does not say how.

Verse 25. And Methuselah lived an hundred eighty and seven years, and begat Lamech:

The oldest mentioned before the firstborn son arrives.

Verse 26. And Methuselah lived after he begat Lamech seven hundred eighty and two years, and begat sons and daughters:

Verse 27. And all the days of Methuselah were nine hundred sixty and nine years: and he died.

The longest life recorded.

Verse 28. And Lamech lived an hundred eighty and two years, and begat a son:

Verse 29. And he called his name Noah, saying, This *same* shall comfort us concerning our work and toil of our hands, because of the ground which the LORD hath cursed.

The first mentioned reference back to Adam

Verse 30. And Lamech lived after he begat Noah five hundred ninety and five years, and begat sons and daughters:

It would appear that Lamech died before the Flood. Presumably, some of Noah's brothers and sisters later drowned in the Flood.

Verse 31. And all the days of Lamech were seven hundred seventy and seven years: and he died.

He seems to have died naturally before the Flood.

Verse 32. And Noah was five hundred years old: and Noah begat Shem, Ham, and Japheth.

Were they triplets? Did they have different mothers or was the five hundred years an approximation?

CHAPTER SIX

Verse 1. AND it came to pass, when men began to multiply on the face of the earth, and daughters were born unto them,

There is a feeling of a change of pace here. It is perhaps interesting that although man was made by God and then woman from a rib, that in birth there can be some male and some female.

Verse 2. That the sons of God saw the daughters of men that they *were* fair; and they took them wives of all which they chose.

This passage would seem to infer that heavenly male beings came down onto the earth and had sexual relationships with earthly women.

Verse 3. And the LORD said, My spirit shall not always strive with man, for that he also *is* flesh: yet his days shall be an hundred and twenty years.

This could be looked at in at least two ways. Either an average life span was to be 120 years of earthly time, or that mankind as a whole might exist on the earth for 120 heavenly years. Is this different from the three score years and ten? (As spoken of in Psalm 90 verse 10.)

Verse 4. There were giants in the earth in those days; and also after that, when the sons of God came in unto the daughters of men, and they bare *children* to them, the same *became* mighty men which *were* of old, men of renown.

These people are obviously different to Adam and Eve. They would appear to be an alien people but in human likeness and able to have normal sexual intercourse with humans. They are larger than earth people and seem to have come from somewhere else in the heavens. They are also referred to as sons of God, but the text does not say why. Do they have something to distinguish them as heavenly?

Verse 5. And GOD saw that the wickedness of man *was* great in the earth, and *that* every imagination of the thoughts of his heart *was* only evil continually.

Man has independent thought conceived in a God given brain and imagination. Did the evil come from those alien beings or was it from the spiritual influence of the devil or evil forces?

Verse 6. And it repented the LORD that he had made man on the earth, and it grieved him at his heart.

This is an extraordinary statement when considered.

Verse 7. And the LORD said, I will destroy man whom I have created from the face of the earth; both

man, and beast, and the creeping thing, and the fowls of the air; for it repenteth me that I have made them.

Each type of life form is considered separately as it was in the creation. God does not appear to consider His creation as simply 'life on earth'. It would appear to read as though God regretted creating all of them.

Verse 8. But Noah found grace in the eyes of the LORD.

Of all creation, God notices one person at least who he can separate from the others. God knows us all individually.

Verse 9. These *are* the generations of Noah: Noah was a just man *and* perfect in his generations, *and* Noah walked with God.

Noah was fair, he came from good stock and he obeyed the ways of the God. Perhaps his family had not been subject to alien interference?

Verse 10. And Noah begat three sons, Shem, Ham, and Japheth.

Enough to start the population again, and it seems all about the same age.

Verse 11. The earth was also corrupt before God, and the earth was filled with violence.

The earth was suffering because of the violence of man. The earth was made to be a beautiful place and God had given the looking after of it to man.

Verse 12. And God looked upon the earth, and, behold, it was corrupt; for all flesh had corrupted his way upon the earth.

Man was spoiling things because he was being selfish rather than working in God's ways.

Verse 13. And God said unto Noah, The end of all flesh is come before me; for the earth is filled with violence through them; and, behold, I will destroy them with the earth.

Time for a clean start. Again we learn that God does not like men to enter into violence. Of all the things that were going on at the time, it is violence that seems to be the most significant to give God displeasure.

Verse 14. Make thee an ark of gopher wood; rooms shalt thou make in the ark, and shalt pitch it within and without with pitch.

Presumably Noah was able to assemble workers and materials. There is also an interesting point architecturally in that rooms were a feature. When one considers the development of buildings, open plan living was the norm for a long time before rooms were created to give privacy.

Verse 15. And this *is the fashion* which thou shalt make it *of:* The length of the ark *shall be* three hundred cubits, the breadth of it fifty cubits, and the height of it thirty cubits.

Four hundred and fifty feet long, seventy five feet wide and forty five feet high, approximately; it was a big boat. It would have needed much wood and perhaps many workers?

Verse 16. A window shalt though make to the ark, and in a cubit shalt thou finish it above; and the door of the ark shalt though set in the side thereof; *with* lower, second, and third *stories* shalt thou make it.

The ark is to have three decks. It must have been very dark inside.

Verse 17. And, behold, I, even I, do bring a flood of waters upon the earth, to destroy all flesh, wherein *is* the breath of life, from under heaven; *and* everything that *is* in the earth shall die.

All the people and creatures not in the ark are to be drowned. Plants and water creatures will presumably survive.

Verse 18. But with thee will I establish my covenant; and thou shalt come into the ark, thou, and thy sons, and thy wife, and thy sons' wives with thee.

There is no mention of either of the younger generation having had children already and it would seem to appear that each man had only one wife. The wives must have also been acceptable to God, to save, as well as Noah and his sons.

Verse 19. And of every living thing of all flesh, two of every *sort* shalt though bring into the ark, to keep *them* alive with thee; they shall be male and female.

God could have scrapped everything and started again but he chose to take some of each sort to restock the earth after the flood.

Verse 20. Of fowls after their kind, and of cattle after their kind, of every creeping thing of the earth after his kind, two of every *sort* shall come unto thee, to keep *them* alive.

It is almost saying that the two animals of each will seek out Noah rather than Noah seeking them. Perhaps it does in fact say that. The choice of the pairs would then have been God's and the animals, thus inspired, would then have gone to the ark.

Verse 21. And take thou unto thee of all food that is eaten, and thou shalt gather *it* to thee; and it shall be for food for thee, and for them.

What a huge job!

Verse 22. Thus did Noah; according to all that God commanded him, so did he.

Noah did what God commanded him and considering all things his faith must have been tried. To build a huge boat when everyone else was carrying on as normal and the sheer amount of time, labour and resources. He was probably being mocked the whole time and if he was using labour other than his own family, then those helping him, were working on a project that was going to be used in the event of them being drowned. An extraordinary situation. Was Noah a boat builder by trade? Did he have a trained staff to help him?

CHAPTER SEVEN

Verse 1. AND the LORD said unto Noah, Come thou and all thy house into the ark; for thee have I seen righteous before me in this generation.

One family, in a whole generation, to be saved from destruction.

Verse 2. Of every clean beast thou shalt take to thee by sevens, the male and his female: and of beasts that *are* not clean by two, the male and his female.

Long before the laws of Moses, we learn that the food laws of what is to be eaten, or not to be eaten, are already formed. Seven pairs of clean beasts go into the ark, it is only the unclean beasts that go in two by two.

Verse 3. Of fowls also of the air by sevens, the male and the female; to keep seed alive upon the face of all the earth.

The spreading of seed via bird droppings and birds as part of the food chain, make birds an essential part of the earth's life system.

Verse 4. For yet seven days, and I will cause it to rain upon the earth forty days and forty nights; and every living substance that I have made will I destroy from off the face of the earth.

Seven days warning.

Verse 5. And Noah did according unto all that the LORD commanded him.

Noah is trusting and faithful. There must have been a lot of people making fun of him.

Verse 6. And Noah *was* six hundred years old when the flood of waters was upon the earth.

This is five years after the death of Lamech, his father.

Verse 7. And Noah went in, and his sons, and his wife, and his sons' wives with him, into the ark, because of the waters of the flood.

It must have been hard. The wives had parents that they had left behind perhaps? There were relatives, friends and possibly also those who had helped to build the ark. It was a very strange situation, this huge boat and all these animals and this family, whilst all the remainder of the world continued their normal lives until the day that the rain started.

Verse 8. Of clean beasts, and of beasts that *are* not clean, and of fowls, and of every thing that creepeth upon the earth,

Every creature was represented that relied upon dry land.

Verse 9. There went in two and two unto Noah into the ark, the male and the female, as God had commanded Noah.

This is a phenomenal operation but perhaps the animals were inspired to be at the best place at the best time and to co-operate.

Verse 10. And it came to pass after seven days, that the waters of the flood were upon the earth.

After seven days of heavy rain the landscape would have been changed considerably, as it still is today in wet periods.

Verse 11. In the sixth hundredth year of Noah's life, in the second month, the seventeenth day of the month, the same day were all the fountains of the

great deep broken up, and the windows of heaven were opened.

Do we have movement of the continental plates with tidal waves and hurricane conditions? There is no mention of wind, just rain. The dating is very specific but then Noah must have been of considerable mental ability to organise the whole operation, or sufficiently open to God's inspiration. Ship's logs are very specific today and Noah was captain of a vast craft with a very unusual cargo.

Verse 12. And the rain was upon the earth forty days and forty nights.

A long time of constant pouring rain.

Verse 13. In the selfsame day entered Noah, and Shem, and Ham, and Japheth, the sons of Noah, and Noah's wife, and the three wives of his sons with them, into the ark;

They were all together. Presumably the sons are listed in order of age. They and Noah have one wife each. There is no mention of servants.

Verse 14. They, and every beast after his kind, and all the cattle after their kind, and every creeping thing that creepeth upon the earth after his kind, and every fowl after his kind, every bird of every sort.

Not just two of every type of animal or bird but two of each variety?

Verse 15. And they went in unto Noah into the ark, two and two of all flesh, wherein *is* the breath of life.

All air breathing creatures.

Verse 16. And they that went in, went in male and female of all flesh, as God had commanded him: and the LORD shut him in.

God was in control and He took care of them.

Verse 17. And the flood was forty days upon the earth; and the waters increased, and bare up the ark, and it was lift up above the earth.

The ark floated.

Verse 18. And the waters prevailed, and were increased greatly upon the earth; and the ark went upon the face of the waters.

The ark now seems to be in full movement.

Verse 19. And the waters prevailed exceedingly upon the earth; and all the high hills, that *were* under the whole heaven, were covered.

Even the hills were covered with water.

Verse 20. Fifteen cubits upward did the waters prevail; and the mountains were covered.

This seems impossible until we consider the mountain ranges under the Pacific Ocean. There may have been a whole realignment of the earth's surface or perhaps a meteorite.

Verse 21. And all flesh died that moved upon the earth, both of fowl, and of cattle, and of beast, and of every creeping thing that creepeth upon the earth, and every man:

All were drowned.

Verse 22. All in whose nostrils *was* the breath of life, of all that *was* in the dry *land,* died.

Water creatures of course could live. There is not any mention of some creatures living in salt water and some in fresh water. Perhaps all of the water was fresh at this time.

Verse 23. And every living substance was destroyed which was upon the face of the ground, both man, and cattle, and the creeping things, and the fowl of the heaven; and they were destroyed from the earth: and Noah only remained *alive,* and they that *were* with him in the ark.

A confirmation that all air breathing and living life was destroyed, except for the inhabitants of the ark.

Verse 24. And the waters prevailed upon the earth an hundred and fifty days.

The flood lasted for about five months.

CHAPTER EIGHT

Verse 1. AND God remembered Noah, and every living thing, and all the cattle that *was* with him in the ark: and God made a wind to pass over the earth, and the waters assuaged;

The rain has stopped and the wind dries up the water. The wind, like the Spirit in the Creation, almost.

Verse 2. The fountains also of the deep and the windows of heaven were stopped, and the rain from heaven was restrained;

If the land mass sunk then the water would have pushed up through the cracks creating fountains. It is also possible that God added water to the earth, which may seem far fetched, but why not?

Verse 3. And the waters returned from off the earth continually: and after the end of the hundred and fifty days the waters were abated.

The change is taking place.

Verse 4. And the ark rested in the seventh month, on the seventeenth day of the month, upon the mountains of Ararat.

The whole mountain range had been covered by water. Noah seems to have kept a ship's log.

Verse 5. And the waters decreased continually until the tenth month: in the tenth *month,* on the first *day* of the month, were the tops of the mountain seen.

It had started raining on the seventeenth day of the second month and it was now the tenth month. This piece is reported from a viewer's point of view.

Verse 6. And it came to pass at the end of forty days, that Noah opened the window of the ark which he had made:

Ventilation must have been complex in order that all the livestock and humans had had enough air to breathe.

Verse 7. And he sent forth a raven, which went forth to and fro, until the waters were dried up from off the earth.

The bird must have come back to the ark to be fed.

Verse 8. Also he sent forth a dove from him, to see if the waters were abated from off the face of the ground;

Perhaps the dove was trained in some way, like a homing pigeon.

Verse 9. But the dove found no rest for the sole of her foot, and she returned unto him into the ark, for the waters *were* on the face of the whole earth: then he put forth his hand, and took her, and pulled her in unto him into the ark.

It is not clear why the raven and then the dove were sent out, but presumably the raven would search for a carnivorous meal and the dove for seed. Neither seem to be accessible.

Verse 10. And he stayed yet other seven days; and again he sent forth the dove out of the ark;

Apparently the same bird and not her mate, perhaps it was nesting time.

Verse 11. And the dove came in to him in the evening; and, lo, in her mouth *was* an olive leaf plucked off: so Noah knew that the waters were abated from off the earth.

Confirmation that the bird was female and that the leaf was freshly plucked, rather than picked up. The vegetation seems to have survived intact.

Verse 12. And he stayed yet other seven days; and sent forth the dove; which returned not again unto him any more.

This bird was on her own, the only bird outside of the ark in the whole world, hopefully her mate found her. In verse three of the previous chapter we are told that there were seven pairs of each bird, rather than the two by two arrangement. I wonder if doves mated for life in Biblical times?

Verse 13. And it came to pass in the six hundredth and first year, in the first *month,* the first *day* of the month, the waters were dried up from off the earth: and Noah removed the covering of the ark, and looked, and, behold, the face of the ground was dry.

It would imply that there was some overall covering protecting the Ark in addition to the main structure, but it did not impede the opening of the portal to allow the birds to fly out.

Verse 14. And in the second month, on the seven and twentieth day of the month, was the earth dried.

The soggy soil was dried out and could be walked upon.

Verse 15. And God spake unto Noah, saying,

Always the personal relationship.

Verse 16. Go forth of the ark, thou, and thy wife, and thy sons, and thy sons' wives with thee.

All together as a family.

Verse 17. Bring forth with thee every living thing that *is* with thee, of all flesh, *both* of fowl, and of cattle,

and of every creeping thing that creepeth up on the earth; that they may breed abundantly in the earth, and be fruitful, and multiply upon the earth.

Even the serpents, one of whose ancestors tempted Eve, were given a new chance. All life has it's place: reproduction is a God given event. Sex is a good act created by God.

Verse 18. And Noah went forth, and his sons, and his wife, and his sons' wives with him:

A brave new start for mankind, the old existence washed clean away.

Verse 19. Every beast, every creeping thing, and every fowl, *and* whatsoever creepeth upon the earth, after their kinds, went forth out of the ark.

The animals remained as individual species, they were not cross bred.

Verse 20. And Noah builded an altar unto the LORD; and took of every clean beast, and of every clean fowl, and offered burnt offerings on the altar.

Again we remember that in Chapter 7. Verse 3. that there were seven pairs of every clean beast but only one pair of each unclean beast. Considering later sacrificial accounts, sheep and cattle would have been amongst the clean variety. The animals were under God's protection and, presumably none of the unclean pairs died before they were able to reproduce, otherwise their species would have died out altogether.

Verse 21. And the LORD smelled a sweet savour; and the LORD said in his heart, I will not again curse the ground any more for man's sake; for the imagination of every man's heart *is* evil from his youth; neither will I again smite any more every thing living, as I have done.

We are accepted for what we are and God makes a covenant with man and his environment.

Verse 22. While the earth remaineth, seedtime and harvest, and cold and heat, and summer and winter, and day and night shall not cease.

Whilst the earth remains we shall enjoy certain stabilities.

CONCLUSIONS

These eight chapters cover the creation and the setting up again for the repopulation of the planet on which we live. Science has come up with many theories of it's own as to how things began, but none of the theories offers a complete answer to the result that we enjoy.

Without God there is no reason for any of the creation to have taken place. It is a basic law of science that matter cannot be created and it cannot be destroyed but it's shape can be changed. What matter in the first place? Why should there be any matter? Why should it suddenly or even slowly decide to change? Without outside influences, it could not change and there would not be any outside influences anyway because they would not exist. Without any substance and without any heat or cold or motion of any kind, nothing would be there. There is, however, something there and we are part of it.

The substance of the universe as we know it and as described within Genesis, has come from somewhere else. The contents of the place occupied by the universe, as we know it today, are not in the same state as they would have been at some time before. In fact we do not know what was in this place, now occupied by the galaxies or even if the place existed. There is certainly no reason known to man for it to exist other than by Divine will.

Theories abound as to how the stars and planets came to be where they are and when this happened, but all the theories rely on the concept of a provision of matter and a time and a place for the action to take place. Logically there is no reason for any of these things to be available in the first place, why should they be, if they had not been made available? So who or what made them available, because according to us who experience them, they are to be seen in some part without the need of any scientific equipment made by man to observe them?

The account in Genesis does provide an answer. It may not be an answer acceptable to those who do not believe in a Divine Creator, but never the less it does present a more complete account than scientists have yet been able to suggest. An inspired account of the creation, inspired by the creator himself who was at the scene, so to speak, could arguably be more reliable than scientific speculation based on little, except the will to provide a Godless answer.

The methods of timings are based on certain constants, but who is to say that those constants can be relied upon. As soon as one theory seems to be proved then another discovery seems to change everything again. The true fact is that no one but God was actually there as an eye witness. For someone who believes in inspiration, then an inspired account has probably more to offer than speculation by those who develop a theory and then look to find evidence to support it and to keep the idea going.

There is a lot within the Genesis narrative that fits in with scientific and archaeological discovery. Future generations may discover that Genesis has a lot more to offer than existing scientific knowledge can yet allow it's supporters to understand. It would seem that the main questions have still to be answered\:

- What is beyond the Universe?
- Who created the space for the occupation of the Universe?
- Who created the matter from which the Universe is made?
- Who created the energy to change that matter?
- For what reason was the matter changed?
- Who created reason?
- What is the point of the existence of any of it?
- Who created life?
- Why should any of it be co-ordinated?
- Where did imagination come from to devise theories about creation?

Two rocks on a beach are not usually able to have thoughts about the concept of God.

Grass is one of the oldest forms of life but it has not yet developed legs or learnt to swim, why should it, it has always been grass, each herb according to it's own kind.

I believe that Genesis has the answer to these questions:—GOD.